**Specific Skill Series**
for Language Arts

Writing Process

**Leveled Books
in Nine Key
Language Arts Skill Areas**

Columbus, OH

The **McGraw·Hill** *Companies*

SRAonline.com

 SRA

Copyright © 2005 by SRA/McGraw-Hill.

Send all inquiries to:
SRA/McGraw-Hill
8787 Orion Place
Columbus, OH 43240-4027

Printed in the United States of America.

ISBN 0-07-601708-7

3 4 5 6 7 8 9 RHR 14 13 12 11 10

GENERAL INFORMATION ON THE WRITING PROCESS

The writing process gives students a systematic approach that they can apply to all types of writing. The five stages of the writing process are outlined below.

- **Prewriting:** Writers get ideas and plan their writing. They select a topic, an audience, and a purpose and use graphic organizers.
- **Drafting:** Writers get their ideas on paper without worrying about mistakes.
- **Revising:** Writers revise by stepping back and reexamining their work. They evaluate their ideas, organization, voice, sentence fluency, and word choice.
- **Editing/Proofreading:** Writers check their writing to make sure it is free of grammatical, spelling, and technical mistakes.
- **Publishing:** Writers formally present their work to a particular audience.

In addition to instruction in the writing process and forms of writing, students need exposure to good models of writing, as well as meaningful feedback on their own writing.

ABOUT *SPECIFIC SKILL SERIES FOR LANGUAGE ARTS*

Specific Skill Series for Language Arts is a companion to *Specific Skill Series,* a supplemental reading program that has been widely recognized for its effectiveness for over thirty years. The two series are designed and organized the same. *Specific Skill Series for Language Arts* consists of discrete units of practice exercises that target and reinforce fundamental language-arts skills. Units in both series are presented in multiple-choice format for standardized test practice.

ABOUT *WRITING PROCESS*

The scope and sequence for Books A through H of *Writing Process* focuses on the five stages of the writing process. The scope and sequence for each book is located on the last page of the book. Each unit includes

- **rule boxes** that explain skills and strategies for each stage of the writing process.
- **models** in each rule box to illustrate the skills and strategies.
- **multiple-choice exercises** for skills practice and reinforcement.

Four **Language Activity Pages** (LAPs) appear in each book. Each LAP is divided into the following four sections and reviews the skills practiced in the preceding units:

Exercising Your Skill reviews key terms and concepts.

Expanding Your Skill provides mixed practice.

Exploring Language shows how the skills apply to real-world contexts by featuring one of six forms of writing: descriptive, narrative, personal, persuasive, expository, and poetry.

Expressing Yourself includes two creative activities related to the skills. One activity is always a Work-with-a-Partner activity to encourage collaborative learning.

SERIES COMPONENTS

- **Student Editions:** Nine books in each level (A–H) focus on nine skill areas: *Grammar, Usage, Mechanics, Spelling, Vocabulary, Sentences, Paragraphs, Writing Process,* and *Research.*

- **Placement Test Books:** One book for each skill area includes diagnostic tests to place students in the correct level.

- **Teacher's Manual:** Primarily an answer key, the *Teacher's Manual* also includes reproducible student worksheets and further information on how to use the program, including classroom management tips.

HOW TO USE *SPECIFIC SKILL SERIES FOR LANGUAGE ARTS*

Placing Students in Levels: The scope and sequence, complexity of skills, and readability in Levels A through H correspond to Grades 1 through 8. Students may, however, be placed in <u>any level</u>. For example, in the second grade, a student who needs remedial work in a specific skill may be placed in Book A, an on-level student who would benefit from skills reinforcement may be placed in Book B, and an advanced student who is ready for enrichment may be placed in Book C or higher. *Placement Tests* help place students in the correct level.

Setting: This series can be used for independent study and one-on-one practice sessions, as well as in small-group and whole-class settings. It is also effective in after-school and summer-school programs.

Getting Started: Students must have notebook paper or copies of reproducible student worksheets (located in the *Teacher's Manual*) before they begin working. Remind students not to write in the books. Students may begin in any unit of any book, depending on the skill practice they need, although it is recommended that they begin with Unit 1. As they work through the units, students should record their answers on notebook paper or on the student worksheets.

Pacing: Students should be encouraged to work at their own pace, completing a few units every day or every other day.

Scoring: Teachers should score units as soon as they have been completed. Then a discussion can be held in which students justify their answer choices.

Internet Use: Some activities, especially those in *Research,* require students to use the Internet. Students' use of the Internet should be monitored closely for content appropriateness and safety.

TO THE STUDENT

Skillful writing takes time. There are helpful steps that writers can follow to make the writing process easier. This book will familiarize you with the stages of the writing process.

In Book E *Writing Process,* you will learn about

- Getting Ideas
- Planning
- Drafting
- Revising
- Editing and Proofreading
- Publishing

After you complete this book, you will understand the importance of thinking about your topic and planning your writing. Different types of organizers can be used to plan different types of writing. For example, the organizer below is a cause-and-effect map. It can help you plan writing that tells about the causes that led to an effect.

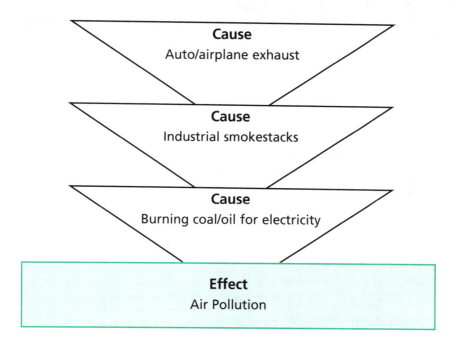

You will also learn to use proofreading marks to label specific errors as you work to improve your writing.

Spelling error: (wheele) ⟶ wheel

Spacing error: The⟍wheel is damaged. ⟶ The wheel is damaged.

Word Order error: Fix⌐wheel⌐the⌐. ⟶ Fix the wheel.

As you master the skills in this book, you will know that following the stages of the writing process will improve your writing.

Unit 1
Getting Ideas

Before you begin to write, you need to **get ideas.** Sometimes a topic is given to you, such as *What I Liked Best about Fourth Grade.* Other times, you get ideas on your own to choose a topic. There are many ways to get ideas: think of things you have done or would like to do, look at your surroundings, think of things you like or do not like, think of stories you have read, talk to friends, or think of your family. In a piece of writing, ideas should be related to, or fit with, the topic.

Which writing idea relates to each topic? If they all relate, choose *All of the above.*

1. **Topic: Things That Are Good for Your Health**
   (A) Fruits and vegetables are nutritious.
   (B) These rollerblades are on sale.
   (C) My chores include taking out the garbage and cleaning my room.
   (D) All of the above

2. **Topic: Reasons to Have a Dog as a Pet**
   (A) A dog can protect its home.
   (B) Dogs make fine companions.
   (C) Caring for a dog teaches responsibility.
   (D) All of the above

3. **Topic: The Civil War**
   (A) Why did the Civil War start?
   (B) Who fought in the Civil War?
   (C) When did the Civil War end?
   (D) All of the above

4. **Topic: Uses of a Computer**
   (A) The library does not have the book I need.
   (B) The CD will be in stores on Tuesday.
   (C) Send an e-mail to a friend who has been absent about homework assignments from your class.
   (D) All of the above

5. **Topic: Sports Played on a Field**
   (A) Field hockey
   (B) Soccer
   (C) Football
   (D) All of the above

6. **Topic: Places to Volunteer**
   (A) My first job was a paper route.
   (B) Parks, hospitals, and libraries
   (C) I am not old enough to work at a restaurant.
   (D) All of the above

7. **Topic: Family Vacation**
   (A) Our family had fun driving across the United States.
   (B) My bicycle needs its front tire fixed.
   (C) My sister likes to play the piano.
   (D) All of the above

8. **Topic: Activities in the Snow**
   (A) Bowling
   (B) Golf
   (C) Snowboarding
   (D) All of the above

9. **Topic: Warm-Weather Activities**
   (A) Snow skiing
   (B) Ice skating
   (C) Boating
   (D) All of the above

10. **Topic: Planning for a Party**
    (A) Guest list
    (B) Invitations
    (C) The party's menu
    (D) All of the above

Unit 1
Getting Ideas

There are different types of writing.

- **Personal writing** such as diary and journal entries reflects who you are. Personal writing such as lists and notes can be practical and useful. It might also include cards, formal and informal letters, and memos.
- **Expository writing** explains how to do something or states facts about something. It includes summaries, reviews, reports, processes, directions, news stories, and some essays.
- **Narrative writing** tells a story. It includes autobiographies, biographies, true stories, historical or science fiction, myths, and plays.

Which idea relates to each type of writing?

11. **Expository Writing: A Science Report**
    - **(A)** Explain what happened to a plant that was not exposed to light.
    - **(B)** Describe how your classroom looks.
    - **(C)** Tell a story about what it might be like to fly.

12. **Narrative Writing: An Autobiography**
    - **(A)** Write about how old you are.
    - **(B)** Write about baking bread.
    - **(C)** Write about the climate in Mexico.

13. **Expository Writing: Directions to the Theater**
    - **(A)** Tell when the telephone was invented.
    - **(B)** Write a list for the grocery store.
    - **(C)** Tell the address of the theater.

14. **Personal Writing: A Business Letter**
    - **(A)** Write about planting seeds.
    - **(B)** Explain what was wrong with the shirt you bought.
    - **(C)** Describe a bridge in the town where you live.

15. **Narrative Writing: Historical Fiction**
    - **(A)** Create a character named Molly, and describe the Boston Tea Party as she saw it.
    - **(B)** Describe your favorite park.
    - **(C)** Explain why newspapers are helpful.

Unit 1
Getting Ideas

- **Descriptive writing** describes. It gives the reader a clearer and more vivid picture of something or someone, such as how something feels, looks, sounds, tastes, or smells. Examples of descriptive writing include descriptions and observation reports, such as a description of a local fair's activities.
- **Persuasive writing** tries to convince people to think or feel a certain way. It should encourage the reader to understand the writer's point of view. Examples of persuasive writing include advertisements, letters to the editor, editorials and editorial cartoons, and persuasive reports.

Which idea relates to each type of writing?

16. **Persuasive Writing: Magazine Advertisement**
- (A) Tell a story about a school field trip.
- (B) Explain how to make a sandwich.
- (C) Tell about a bookstore that has more books at cheaper prices.

17. **Descriptive Writing: Observing Cats Play**
- (A) Write about what cats do with their tails.
- (B) Write a list of what to pack for a camping trip.
- (C) Explain how to get to the post office.

18. **Persuasive Writing: Poster**
- (A) Explain how to fix a flat tire.
- (B) Explain the benefits of recycling.
- (C) Tell where the Arctic Ocean is.

19. **Descriptive Writing: An Outdoor Description**
- (A) Write a thank-you note.
- (B) Write about a rainbow you have seen.
- (C) Explain the plot of a movie.

20. **Persuasive Writing: Letter to the Editor**
- (A) Write about today's weather.
- (B) Write a list of characters in a play.
- (C) Tell why a new shopping mall should not be built.

After you have a topic and get ideas, it is time to **plan** your writing.

- Think of your **audience,** the person or people who will read or hear your writing. A goal of good writing is to connect with the audience. Here are questions to consider: *What does my audience already know about the topic? How can I share my ideas in an appealing way? Do I need to adjust my language or vocabulary for my audience?*

- When you plan your writing, make sure you have a clear **purpose.** Purpose is the reason, or why, you are writing. Sometimes writing has more than one purpose; however, your main purpose should be clear. Your purpose for writing can be to inform, describe, entertain, persuade, convince, or explain.

Read each piece of writing. Then answer the questions that follow.

Our school has recently changed its dress code. We, the students, will now be required to wear uniforms. I think this is a very good idea for many reasons. Wearing uniforms means less time will be spent getting ready for school in the morning. Instead of choosing an outfit or worrying about what others might think of an outfit, we'll simply put on our required uniform. Uniforms can help families save money because a child will not need numerous items of clothing, especially new and expensive items. Also, people will need to visit only one store to find and buy the uniforms. Some people might think that a uniform takes away a student's identity. I think uniforms do just the opposite. They remove the unnecessary attention some clothes receive and allow us to focus on a person's qualities. People are who they are, not what they wear.

1. Who is the most likely audience for this piece of writing?
   (A) people who make school uniforms
   (B) classmates at this student's school
   (C) employees who sell school uniforms

2. What is the main purpose of this piece of writing?
   (A) to convince
   (B) to entertain
   (C) to describe

Bald eagles are a majestic species. They are not actually bald, but their heads and necks are white, giving them a bald-like appearance. Bald eagles have proud faces with hooked beaks and, typically, golden eyes. Adults can grow to a height of three feet and a weight of fifteen pounds. Feathers on their bodies are brown or black with light-colored tips. Bald eagles have powerful feet with sharp talons. These birds are very graceful as they fly. Adults can have wingspans up to seven feet long.

3. Who is the most likely audience for this piece of writing?
(A) the writer's friends
(B) the writer's sister
(C) the writer's teacher

4. What is the main purpose of this piece of writing?
(A) to describe
(B) to persuade
(C) to entertain

To Whom It May Concern:

I am writing about your company's Xact 900 camera, which I recently bought from Quest Camera Shop. The purchase date and location are on the enclosed receipt. My developed photos came back blurry. Upon inspection, a store employee showed me a defect in the camera lens. Store policy states that exchanges are made directly by your company. I have included the required information to process my request. Please let me know if you need anything else to complete the exchange.

Thank you,

Shevon Roberts

5. Who is the most likely audience for this piece of writing?
(A) an employee at the camera company
(B) the writer's family
(C) an employee at Quest Camera Shop

6. What is the main purpose of this piece of writing?
(A) to entertain   (B) to explain   (C) to convince

Once you have a topic and have considered the audience and purpose for a piece of writing, the next step is to develop a **thesis.** A thesis is a sentence that clearly states the main idea of a piece of writing. It helps the audience understand what the writer is trying to accomplish. The thesis also focuses the writer. Ask yourself: *What is my point? What am I trying to say?* The thesis is then supported throughout the piece of writing by such things as details, facts, and, at times, the writer's opinions.

Which thesis supports each topic?

7. **Topic: The Art of Glass Blowing**
   (A) Baskets are used for practical and decorative purposes.
   (B) There are many types of pans you can use in an oven.
   (C) Craftspeople have been creating shapely glass art for centuries.

8. **Topic: Camels**
   (A) There are two types of camels.
   (B) Zoos provide opportunities to view animals from near and far.
   (C) I feed my fish at the same time every day.

9. **Topic: The Solar System**
   (A) Papermaking is an interesting process.
   (B) Vermont is part of the region of the United States known as New England.
   (C) Our solar system includes nine known planets.

10. **Topic: Racecars**
    (A) Home delivery of the newspaper is convenient and reliable.
    (B) A road atlas is essential when driving across the country.
    (C) With so many cars, the world of racing entertains a diverse audience.

11. **Topic: College Preparation**
    (A) Hobbies are a good way to meet people and make new friends.
    (B) It is valuable to visit colleges before deciding which to attend.
    (C) There are many steps to designing a landscape.

12. **Topic: Skyscrapers**
    (A) The term *skyscraper* is thought to have originated in 1883.
    (B) Earth is divided into hemispheres.
    (C) San Francisco is one American city with an active trolley system.

13. **Topic: Remodeling Your Home**

(A) School bus stops should be at safe and accessible locations.

(B) Creating a list of priorities is helpful if you are remodeling.

(C) Our neighborhood is organizing a community yard sale.

14. **Topic: President James A. Garfield**

(A) Congress includes the Senate and the House of Representatives.

(B) The United States Senate consists of one hundred members.

(C) James A. Garfield was the twentieth president of the United States.

15. **Topic: Buying a Video Camera**

(A) Most magazines print letters to the editor in a special section.

(B) It is important to know which features you need in a video camera.

(C) There are many Native American tribes with their own languages.

16. **Topic: Becoming a Chef**

(A) Elegant restaurants typically require reservations.

(B) Institutes around the world train chefs in different cuisines.

(C) Camping is permitted in designated areas only.

17. **Topic: Comic Books**

(A) Science fiction and superheroes are widespread in comic books.

(B) The classifieds are a popular portion of most newspapers.

(C) The novel's theme addresses how some risks can be worthwhile.

18. **Topic: How to Make Cheese**

(A) Based on the kind of cheese, there are several phases of preparation.

(B) Pancake and waffle flavors are not limited to blueberry.

(C) Employees at a bakery normally work while most of us sleep.

19. **Topic: American Architects**

(A) The Olympics receive worldwide media coverage.

(B) Although born in America, an architect can have international influence.

(C) Years of schooling are required to become a lawyer.

20. **Topic: What is a Kookaburra?**

(A) Common building materials include concrete, steel, and wood.

(B) Some species of trees can thrive for hundreds of years.

(C) A kookaburra is a bird native to Australia and Tasmania.

With the thesis written, a **graphic organizer** can now be used to map information to support the thesis. Graphic organizers are a visual way to plan the main points for a piece of writing. They can also help a writer decide what is or is not important to the thesis. There are many organizers to fit different purposes. Here are some examples:

- A **Venn diagram** compares two related subjects.
- A **web** organizes a main topic, subtopics, and details for each subtopic.
- A **story map** plans the necessary elements of a story.
- A **cause-and-effect map** shows the causes that lead to a result.
- A **time line** shows events in the order they happened.

Which graphic organizer would work best to plan each writing assignment?

21. Ramon plans to write about the construction of the Hoover Dam.
    (A) story map
    (B) time line
    (C) Venn diagram

22. Elizabeth plans to write about the bad effects of pollution.
    (A) web
    (B) cause-and-effect map
    (C) story map

23. Kristin plans to write a science report about cactus growth.
    (A) cause-and-effect map
    (B) story map
    (C) Venn diagram

24. Theo plans to write a summary of a news article's main points.
    (A) Venn diagram
    (B) cause-and-effect map
    (C) web

25. Rosa plans to compare black and brown bears in her report.
    (A) cause-and-effect map
    (B) Venn diagram
    (C) time line

26. Akira plans to write a story based on his pets.
    (A) story map
    (B) web
    (C) Venn diagram

27. Heath plans to write about household issues and ways to fix them.
    (A) Venn diagram
    (B) story map
    (C) cause-and-effect map

28. Winona plans to write about the order of events in the campaign of President Carter.
    (A) time line
    (B) web
    (C) Venn diagram

29. Cole plans to compare hot-air and regular balloons in his report.
    (A) Venn diagram
    (B) cause-and-effect map
    (C) web

30. Josephine plans to write a letter to the editor with details about her school's new gym.
    (A) story map
    (B) web
    (C) Venn diagram

31. Alissa plans to write about the causes of a tornado.
    (A) web
    (B) cause-and-effect map
    (C) time line

32. Marvin plans to write an autobiography that begins at age six.
    (A) cause-and-effect map
    (B) Venn diagram
    (C) time line

Unit 3
Drafting

After you plan your writing, turn your ideas into sentences and paragraphs during the **drafting** phase. Information in a graphic organizer can be used this way. Start by writing a **topic sentence.**

Many cities in the world have populations in the millions.

Then write **supporting details,** or sentences that tell about the topic. With more than thirty-five million people, Tokyo, Japan, is the world's largest city. The city of New York has more than twenty-one million people. Sao Paulo, Brazil, has nearly twenty million people.

Develop a **closing sentence** that reflects the purpose of your writing. At this growth rate, we need to be sensible with natural resources.

Read each Venn diagram. Which is the correct way to turn the diagram's information into sentences?

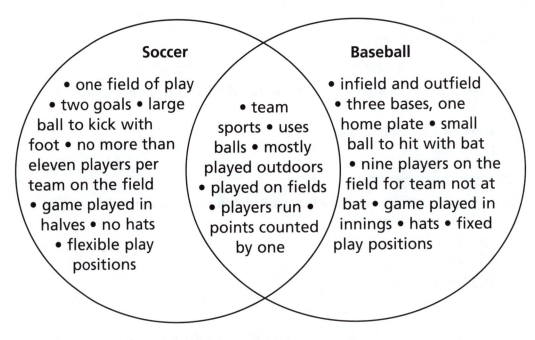

Soccer
- one field of play
- two goals • large ball to kick with foot • no more than eleven players per team on the field • game played in halves • no hats • flexible play positions

- team sports • uses balls • mostly played outdoors • played on fields • players run • points counted by one

Baseball
- infield and outfield
- three bases, one home plate • small ball to hit with bat • nine players on the field for team not at bat • game played in innings • hats • fixed play positions

1. **(A)** Baseball and soccer are very different, but they do share some similarities. Both are team sports that use a type of ball. Baseball and soccer are mostly played outdoors. If it is a goal in soccer or a run in baseball, each is worth a score of one.

   (B) Baseball and soccer are very different, but they do share some similarities. Soccer has an infield and an outfield. There are six infield players and three outfielders. Each baseball team has its own goal. Soccer has referees, and baseball has umpires.

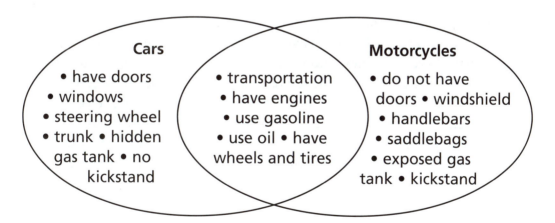

Dogs

- bark and growl
- can protect
- poor climbers
- bigger teeth
- bigger noses
- bigger ears

- good companions
- have fur • have four legs • have tails • sensitive hearing

Cats

- meow and purr
- cannot protect
- great climbers
- smaller teeth
- smaller noses
- smaller ears

2. **(A)**   Dogs and cats are great pets. Many people prefer one over the other. There are many breeds of dogs and cats. While dogs are good climbers, cats are even better at protecting their homes.

    (B)   Dogs and cats are great pets. Many people prefer one or the other. Both animals can be good companions. They both hear and sense things that humans cannot. Cats are more flexible than dogs and can climb just about anything. Many dogs can protect, but cats cannot.

Cars

- have doors
- windows
- steering wheel
- trunk • hidden gas tank • no kickstand

- transportation
- have engines
- use gasoline
- use oil • have wheels and tires

Motorcycles

- do not have doors • windshield
- handlebars
- saddlebags
- exposed gas tank • kickstand

3. **(A)**   Cars and motorcycles are modes of transportation. Cars don't have windows, but at least you can see their gas tanks. A motorcycle has a hidden gas tank and no trunk. Motorcycles can have sidecars.

    (B)   Cars and motorcycles are modes of transportation. Both of them use gasoline; however, a car's gas tank is hidden, whereas a motorcycle's tank is exposed. For steering, a car uses a wheel, but a motorcycle requires the use of handlebars.

Read each web. Which is the best way to turn the web's information into sentences?

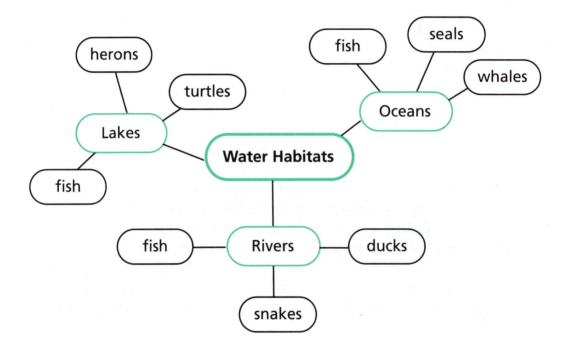

4. **(A)** There are different types of water habitats. Most water habitats have a variety of animals living in them. For example, lakes often have herons, turtles, and fish. In a river, you might find fish, snakes, and ducks. You also can see fish, seals, and whales in oceans.

(B) There are different types of water habitats. They all have different species of animals. In a river you can see seals, and, if it is deep enough, a whale. Lakes often attract a variety of snakes. They make a splendid meal for the herons when they leave their native rivers in search of food.

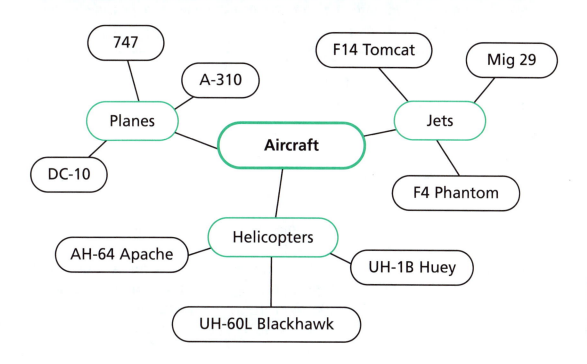

5. **(A)**   The term *aircraft* is not limited to airplanes. For example, a UH-1B Huey is a type of jet, as is a DC-10. Helicopters, such as the F4 Phantom also fall into this category. As far as planes go, there are Mig 29s and the AH-64 Apaches.

   (B)   The term *aircraft* is not limited to airplanes. It includes planes, jets, and helicopters. Some aircraft are commercial, or for public use, but many aircraft are only for the military. Some well-known planes are the DC-10, 747, and A-310. Military jets have interesting names, such as F14 Tomcats and F4 Phantoms. Military helicopters include the AH-64 Apache, UH-1B Huey, and the UH-60L Blackhawk.

Information found on time lines and in cause-and-effect maps can also be turned into sentences and paragraphs.

Read each time line. Which is the correct way to turn the time line's information into sentences?

Jesse Owens

1913	1922	1928	1935	1936
born in Oakville, Alabama	family moved to Cleveland, Ohio	set junior high school world records in the high and long (known then as *broad*) jumps	tied one world record and set three others while a student athlete at The Ohio State University	won four Olympic gold medals

1. **(A)** In 1913 Jesse Owens was born in Oakville, Alabama. At the age of nine, Jesse and his family moved to Cleveland, Ohio. Jesse began to excel in track and field during junior high, setting world records in 1928. After continued high school success, his next destination was The Ohio State University. At a 1935 track meet in Ann Arbor, Michigan, Jesse set more world records. In 1936 he ran to fame by winning four Olympic gold medals.

   (B) Jesse Owens won four gold medals in the 1928 Olympics. He was born in Alabama in 1922. In 1933, while attending The Ohio State University, Jesse set world records in track and field. While in high school, he set his first world records. He went on to win six Olympic gold medals in 1936.

Unit 4
Drafting

Five of the Original Colonies

1607	1620	1636	1638	1653
Virginia	Massachusetts	Rhode Island	Delaware	North Carolina

2. **(A)**   It is difficult to know for sure when each of the thirteen American colonies was settled. We do know that Virginia was the first colony settled in 1620. Delaware wasn't too far behind when it was settled in 1636. Rhode Island followed in 1653.

   (B)   It is difficult to know for sure when each of the thirteen American colonies was settled. In 1607 Virginia became the first colony. Massachusetts was founded in 1620. People from many lands settled in the New World. Rhode Island was settled in 1636, and Delaware followed in 1638. In 1653 North Carolina became the only new colony of that decade.

Sally Ride

1951	1973	1975	1978	1983
born on May 26 in Encino, California	earned bachelor degree from Stanford University	earned master of science degree in physics	completed doctorate degree in physics	became the first American woman in space

3. **(A)**   Sally Ride was born in 1955. In 1975 she graduated from Stanford University. It would be almost 10 years until she would become the first woman in space in 1983.

   (B)   Sally Ride was born in 1951. She earned bachelor, master, and doctorate degrees at Stanford. In 1983 she was the first American woman in space.

Read each cause-and-effect map. Which is the best way to turn the map's information into sentences?

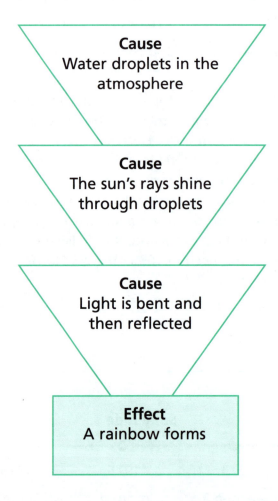

Cause
Water droplets in the atmosphere

Cause
The sun's rays shine through droplets

Cause
Light is bent and then reflected

Effect
A rainbow forms

4. **(A)**   One of nature's beautiful sights is a rainbow. The way a rainbow forms is not as complicated as we might think. First, drops of water must be present in the atmosphere. Then, at a certain position, rays of sunlight must shine through the drops of water. What needs to happen next is, perhaps, the hardest part to explain. The rays are refracted, or bent, and then reflected as the colors we see.

(B)   Have you ever wondered how a rainbow is formed? When the sun's rays shine through clouds, the light is absorbed by the atmosphere. Then the light travels on tiny molecules in the atmosphere. Once they turn a certain temperature, the molecules erupt into a rainbow of color. Because the molecules are heavier than the oxygen in the atmosphere, they bend, forming a bow-like structure.

Cause
The French had claimed nearly 830,000 acres of land west of the Mississippi River

Cause
France needed funds to continue their fight against Britain

Cause
President Thomas Jefferson wanted to buy New Orleans as a port

Effect
The Louisiana Purchase

5. (A) The Louisiana Purchase happened when President Thomas Jefferson wanted to buy New Orleans as a port. France needed money to keep fighting Britain and Ireland, so they were more than happy to sell this land. It was land that Spain had originally claimed in 1798 on an expedition. Spanish explorers were quick to sign the property over to France once they realized their treasure lay elsewhere.

(B) Sometimes an offer is just too good to refuse. On behalf of President Thomas Jefferson, James Monroe and Robert Livingston traveled to France to negotiate the purchase of New Orleans as a port. However, France was fighting a costly war against Britain. Napoleon wished to sell the territory France called Louisiana to help fund the war. With a price of fifteen million dollars set, Monroe and Livingston returned to the United States, having nearly doubled its size.

A. Exercising Your Skill

You have been learning about different types of writing, how to get writing ideas, how to plan your writing, and how to develop a thesis. You have learned about audience and purpose. You have also learned about several graphic organizers and how their information can be changed into topic sentences, supporting details, and closing sentences. Number your paper from 1 to 12. Read each sentence below to decide if it is true or false. If the sentence is true, write the letter **T** on your paper. If it is false, write the letter **F.**

1. The first thing to do for a piece of writing is develop its thesis.

2. Ideas in a piece of writing should be related to its topic.

3. Personal writing explains a process.

4. Narrative writing tells a story.

5. Expository writing asks people to think or feel a certain way.

6. An example of persuasive writing is a magazine advertisement.

7. Descriptive writing should provide a vivid picture for the reader.

8. Audience is the reason a person writes.

9. A thesis should clearly state a piece of writing's main idea.

10. All graphic organizers are the same, without different purposes.

11. Supporting details do not tell about a piece of writing's topic.

12. A closing sentence should reflect a piece of writing's purpose.

B. Expanding Your Skill

Think of the different graphic organizers you have studied. Think about their purposes. Number your paper from 1 to 5. Match each graphic organizer to the writing assignment it would plan best.

Writing Assignment	Graphic Organizer
1. a story about living on the moon	(A) time line
2. the construction of the Brooklyn Bridge	(B) Venn diagram
3. the cause of World War I	(C) cause-and-effect map
4. a summary of a poem	(D) web
5. compare emus and ostriches	(E) story map

C. Exploring Language

Expository Writing Number your paper from 1 to 5. Read the passage below to answer the questions that follow.

A grilled cheese sandwich is quick and easy to make with many choices. Choose the type of bread and cheeses you like. Remember, some cheeses melt better than others. Get what you need to make one sandwich: two bread slices, two cheese slices, butter, a frying pan and its lid, a butter knife, and a spatula. Set out the cheese to reach room temperature; it should melt easier. Butter one side of each bread slice. This helps brown the sandwich and keeps it from sticking to the pan. With an adult's help, preheat the pan on the stove using a low setting. Put the cheese between the bread, buttered sides facing out. Use the spatula to carefully place the sandwich in the pan. On a medium setting, watch as one side browns. Flip the sandwich and repeat. If the cheese has not melted enough, turn off the stove, and put the lid on the pan. The cheese should melt in a few minutes. Use the spatula to remove the sandwich, let it cool, and enjoy!

1. Which graphic organizer would have planned this passage best?
   (A) Venn diagram   (B) web

2. Who is the most likely audience for this passage?
   (A) a cooking class   (B) an art class

3. What is the main purpose of this passage?
   (A) to entertain   (B) to explain

4. What is the underlined sentence in this passage?
   (A) supporting detail   (B) topic sentence

5. Does the underlined sentence reflect the writer's purpose?
   (A) Yes   (B) No

D. Expressing Yourself

Choose one of these activities. When you are finished, give your paper to your teacher.

1. Think of two animals to compare, such as a giraffe and a zebra. Use a Venn diagram to list the similarities and differences of the animals.

2. **WORK with a PARTNER** With a partner, think of a product to sell. Design a persuasive poster or advertisement to show and explain the product.

Unit 5
Revising

After you write, it is time to **revise.** This is when you improve your writing and make it clearer. Here are two ways to start revising.
- Add more details, facts, or sentences to support the main idea.
- Remove details, facts, or sentences that do *not* support the main idea.

Once you have added or removed information, make sure your writing stays on topic. Always keep in mind the purpose of your writing.

Read each passage. Then answer the questions about how to revise it.

In my town, there is a wonderful park named the Park of Roses. It occupies many acres of land and offers much to do. My neighborhood has many bike paths. The park includes a public library, a recreation center, a playground, and tennis courts. There are also basketball courts and baseball diamonds. With all that, the park still has plenty of room to walk dogs, have picnics, or toss a football. Soccer fields and an ice-skating pond are situated near the back of the park by the river. Another area has a shelter and picnic tables. It can be used for various gatherings. Opposite the shelter is the reason for the park's name, a lovely rose garden. Benches and a gazebo allow visitors to relax and enjoy the roses.

1. Which supporting detail should be added to the passage?
   (A) The traffic light at the end of my street is broken.
   (B) I have never ice-skated outdoors.
   (C) Though other parks in town have roses, none have as many.

2. Which closing sentence should be added to the passage?
   (A) This library is one of the largest in the region.
   (B) There used to be a place in the park to play horseshoes.
   (C) The Park of Roses is a terrific resource for the community.

3. Which sentence should be removed from the passage?
   (A) My neighborhood has many bike paths.
   (B) It occupies many acres of land and offers much to do.
   (C) There are also basketball courts and baseball diamonds.

Benjamin Franklin had many interests. Born in 1706 he was the fifteenth child in his family. By 1730 Benjamin Franklin ran a printing company. Pennsylvania entered the Union in 1787. Retired from business in 1748 Franklin divided his time between science and politics.

4. Which supporting detail should be added to the passage?
   (A) Thomas Jefferson and George Washington grew up in Virginia.
   (B) An image of Abraham Lincoln is on the five-dollar bill.
   (C) Franklin was a publisher, an inventor, and a philosopher.

5. Which closing sentence should be added to the passage?
   (A) The Declaration of Independence was signed on July 4, 1776.
   (B) By balancing his interests, Franklin greatly contributed to society.
   (C) The Constitutional Convention of 1787 was held in Philadelphia.

6. Which sentence should be removed from the passage?
   (A) Pennsylvania entered the Union in 1787.
   (B) By 1730 Benjamin Franklin ran a printing company.
   (C) Benjamin Franklin had many interests.

Red pandas are related to giant pandas. They are smaller with reddish-black fur. Carnivores eat meat. Red pandas have white and black face marks and light tail rings. Tails help them balance while climbing.

7. Which supporting detail should be added to the passage?
   (A) Bamboo leaves are a major part of the red panda's diet.
   (B) Herbivores eat plants.
   (C) The Himalayan mountains extend through southern Asia.

8. Which closing sentence should be added to the passage?
   (A) Many other animals have distinct markings on their face.
   (B) Omnivores eat both meat and plants.
   (C) Red pandas, like their relatives, are shy and keep to themselves.

9. Which sentence should be removed from the passage?
   (A) Red pandas are related to giant pandas.
   (B) Carnivores eat meat.
   (C) Red pandas have white and black face marks and light tail rings.

Read each passage. Then answer the questions about how to revise it.

A Venus flytrap is a plant that originates from North Carolina. It grows in humid areas. Bright light and soil with a high acid level help Venus flytraps thrive. Venus is the name of one planet in the solar system. What makes this plant unique is that it eats insects, thus the term *flytrap* in its name. A Venus flytrap has jaw-like leaves to close upon its prey. The leaves have sensitive hairs. When an insect lands on them, the hairs act as a trigger to shut the plant's leaves, or "trap." Then the insect cannot escape, and the plant slowly digests it.

10. Which supporting detail should be added to the passage?
(A) Some spiders have very large, round bodies.
(B) A Venus flytrap has leaves that smell sweet to attract insects.
(C) There are numerous insects smaller than flies.

11. Which sentence should be removed from the passage?
(A) A Venus flytrap has jaw-like leaves to close upon its prey.
(B) Bright light and soil with a high acid level help Venus flytraps thrive.
(C) Venus is the name of one planet in the solar system.

Have you ever wondered about the history of pizza? It can actually be traced back to ancient times. Greeks, Romans, and some Middle Eastern cultures ate a pizza-like flat bread. However, Naples, Italy, is credited with the version of pizza we know today. It is believed that green basil, white mozzarella cheese, and red tomatoes were put on flat bread to represent the colors of Italy's flag. The flag of Madagascar also includes green, white, and red. In the early 1900s, Italian immigrants brought the tradition of pizza with them to America.

12. Which supporting detail should be added to the passage?
(A) Madagascar is an island off the southeastern coast of Africa.
(B) Modena, Maranello, and Milan are all cities in Italy.
(C) Some ancient cultures topped their flat bread with oil and spices.

13. Which sentence should be removed from the passage?
(A) The flag of Madagascar also includes green, white, and red.
(B) Have you ever wondered about the history of pizza?
(C) It can actually be traced back to ancient times.

The Grand Canyon is located in northwest Arizona, bordering Utah and Nevada. The Colorado River flows through the canyon. Because of this, the canyon is often measured in river miles. The Grand Canyon, by this measurement, is 277 miles long. From its rim to the river, the canyon is more than a mile high. Its width ranges between ten and eighteen miles. The Escalante River is in Utah. We have the Colorado River to thank for the stunning Grand Canyon. For centuries, the river has chiseled and shaped it.

14. Which supporting detail should be added to the passage?
    (A) Canyon walls consist of minerals, and iron is its most common.
    (B) The western United States has many campground areas.
    (C) The western United States is home to diverse wildlife.

15. Which sentence should be removed from the passage?
    (A) The Grand Canyon, by this measurement, is 277 miles long.
    (B) The Escalante River is in Utah.
    (C) From its rim to the river, the canyon is more than a mile high.

Cubism is an example of an art movement. The main trait of Cubism is its use of geometric forms to represent an artist's subject. It is also important that multiple points of view are shown at the same time. Cubism developed in three phases. The first phase dates back to 1907. This abstract movement was started by two artists who shared similar influences, Pablo Picasso and Georges Braque. Mary Cassatt followed the art movement known as Impressionism. Cubism is thought to have inspired other art movements, such as Futurism.

16. Which supporting detail should be added to the passage?
    (A) Algebra and geometry are examples of mathematics.
    (B) Born in 1844 Mary Cassatt was an American artist.
    (C) Like Cubism, Futurism features fragmented forms.

17. Which sentence should be removed from the passage?
    (A) Mary Cassatt followed the art movement known as Impressionism.
    (B) Cubism is an example of an art movement.
    (C) The first phase dates back to 1907.

Read each passage. Then answer the questions about how to revise it.

The Boston Marathon in Massachusetts has a long history. John Graham managed the Boston Athletic Association's running team that won six Olympic gold medals in 1896. This inspired him to organize an annual long-distance race. Today many other cities across the country have marathons. With the help of other Boston Athletic Association members and businessman Herbert H. Holt, the first Boston Marathon occurred on April 19, 1897. The marathon's length was 24.5 miles. In 1924 the length increased slightly in order to meet Olympic standards.

18. Which supporting detail should be added to the passage?
   (A) The 1900 Olympics were held in Paris, France.
   (B) Fifteen runners participated in the first Boston Marathon.
   (C) Athens is a city in Greece.

19. Which sentence should be removed from the passage?
   (A) The Boston Marathon in Massachusetts has a long history.
   (B) Today many other cities across the country have marathons.
   (C) The marathon's length was 24.5 miles.

Have you ever heard of Groundhog Day? Stemming from a German tradition, the earliest American record of Groundhog Day is 1841. Groundhog Day, however, was not celebrated officially until February 2, 1886. Legend has it that if a groundhog comes out of its hole and casts a shadow, there will be six more weeks of winter. Squirrels bury acorns so they have food to eat throughout the winter. Perhaps the most famous groundhog is Punxsutawney Phil. Each February 2 people wait for the Pennsylvanian groundhog to appear.

20. Which supporting detail should be added to the passage?
   (A) If the groundhog does not cast a shadow, then spring will arrive early.
   (B) Chipmunks are members of the squirrel family.
   (C) The capital of Pennsylvania is Harrisburg.

21. Which sentence should be removed from the passage?
   (A) Have you ever heard of Groundhog Day?
   (B) Perhaps the most famous groundhog is Punxsutawney Phil.
   (C) Squirrels bury acorns so they have food to eat throughout the winter.

Ice-skating sensation Kristi Yamaguchi was born in California on July 12, 1971. As an amateur figure skater, Kristi achieved great success. Most notably, Kristi and her skating partner Rudy Galindo placed first in the 1988 World Junior Championships and the 1989 and 1990 U.S.A. Nationals. Kristi eventually focused all of her skating energy into singles competition. Tennis players can compete in singles and doubles. After winning an Olympic gold medal in 1992, Kristi left her amateur rank behind to turn professional in 1993.

22. Which supporting detail should be added to the passage?
(A) Kristi was the ladies' singles world champion in 1991 and 1992.
(B) Roller-skating is not an Olympic event.
(C) Tennis can be played on different surfaces.

23. Which sentence should be removed from the passage?
(A) As an amateur figure skater, Kristi achieved great success.
(B) Tennis players can compete in singles and doubles.
(C) Kristi eventually focused all of her skating energy into singles competition.

Do you know what an Ohio Buckeye is? Aside from being a college mascot, an Ohio Buckeye is a tree. *Buckeye* is the name of the nut that the tree produces. It is thought that Native Americans gave the buckeye this name because it looks likes the eye of a male deer, or a buck. The tree itself can grow thirty to fifty feet tall. The tree's trunk can be two to three feet around. The state tree of New Hampshire is the white birch. The buckeye tree's bark is gray and, when it blooms, the tree's flowers are white to greenish-yellow.

24. Which supporting detail should be added to the passage?
(A) The state tree of Minnesota is the red pine.
(B) Buckeye nuts are a glossy, dark brown with a lighter brown "eye."
(C) The state flower of Ohio is the scarlet carnation.

25. Which sentence should be removed from the passage?
(A) Buckeye is the name of the nut that the tree produces.
(B) The tree's trunk can be two to three feet around.
(C) The state tree of New Hampshire is the white birch.

Unit 6
Revising

As you revise, make sure your writing is organized correctly. Ask yourself if your ideas, details, facts, and sentences are in the **correct order.** For example, when writing a story, you would not wait until the end to introduce the story's characters. Or, when explaining a process, you would explain the steps in the order they occur.

Incorrect: I like to make my own salad. I add salad dressing and toss all the ingredients. Finally, I add shredded cheese and nuts or croutons. First, I wash the vegetables and then chop them.

Correct: I like to make my own salad. First, I wash the vegetables and then chop them. I add salad dressing and toss all the ingredients. Finally, I add shredded cheese and nuts or croutons.

Which group of sentences is in the correct order?

1. **(A)** Hurricanes are the most powerful of all storms. A hurricane begins to develop when winds from different directions converge above a tropical ocean. The winds swirl in a circular pattern, and a large low-pressure system forms in the center. The winds rotate faster and faster as they move toward land, gathering vast amounts of water that create gigantic waves.

   (B) The winds swirl in a circular pattern, and a large low-pressure system forms in the center. Hurricanes are the most powerful of all storms. A hurricane begins to develop when winds from different directions converge above a tropical ocean. The winds rotate faster and faster as they move toward land, gathering vast amounts of water that create gigantic waves.

2. **(A)** They made art that was more realistic than what previous artists created. Renaissance artists rediscovered the classical beauty typical of ancient Greece and Rome. The Renaissance produced beautiful artwork. In fact, some art experts believe that the works of Leonardo da Vinci and Michelangelo are the most perfect representations of the human form ever created.

   (B) The Renaissance produced beautiful artwork. Renaissance artists rediscovered the classical beauty typical of ancient Greece and Rome. They made art that was more realistic than what previous artists created. In fact, some art experts believe that the works of Leonardo da Vinci and Michelangelo are the most perfect representations of the human form ever created.

3. (A)   Before planting a vegetable garden, it helps to plan its layout. Label each vegetable and where it is planted. Consider how much space each plant should need. List the vegetables you plan to grow. Remember to plant from tallest to shortest, where the tallest plants are at the rear of the garden. Buy the seeds and any other items you need.

  (B)   Before planting a vegetable garden, it helps to plan its layout. List the vegetables you plan to grow. Consider how much space each plant should need. Buy the seeds and any other items you need. Label each vegetable and where it is planted. Remember to plant from tallest to shortest, where the tallest plants are at the rear of the garden.

4. (A)   There is a frog that lives in a piano at school. We named the frog Naomi. Naomi tried to keep her whereabouts a secret, but a croak or a ribbit could be heard every time someone played the piano. Naomi would quickly hide when anyone tried to find her. One day Naomi returned from her daily swim to find that her entrance into the piano was blocked. Now the trombone sure sounds a lot like a frog.

  (B)   Naomi would quickly hide when anyone tried to find her. We named the frog Naomi. There is a frog that lives in a piano at school. Now the trombone sure sounds a lot like a frog. One day Naomi returned from her daily swim to find that her entrance into the piano was blocked. Naomi tried to keep her whereabouts a secret, but a croak or a ribbit could be heard every time someone played the piano.

5. (A)   Helicopters are not the fastest type of aircraft, but they are versatile. Helicopters can move up and down, backward and forward, and side to side. By remaining still, helicopters can hover in the air. They can fly very low above land or water also. Helicopters can take off and land in very small areas. Unlike airplanes, helicopters do not even need a runway for take-off or landing.

  (B)   Unlike airplanes, helicopters do not even need a runway for take-off or landing. By remaining still, helicopters can hover in the air. Helicopters can move up and down, backward and forward, and side to side. Helicopters are not the fastest type of aircraft, but they are versatile. Helicopters can take off and land in very small areas. They can fly very low above land or water also.

Read each paragraph. Then choose the paragraph in which the circled sentence has been moved to show the correct order.

6. (A) They are expert swimmers and divers that spend most of their time in water. (Otters are agile mammals.) An otter's streamlined body, strong legs, and waterproof coat enable it to swim quickly and easily. An otter's tail and webbed hind feet help it navigate in water. Otters eat various sea life. Otter whiskers help them sense small animals in murky water, as well as avoid obstacles while swimming. Otters have small front paws, which they use to hold their food when they eat.

(B) They are expert swimmers and divers that spend most of their time in water. (Otters are agile mammals.) An otter's streamlined body, strong legs, and waterproof coat enable it to swim quickly and easily. An otter's tail and webbed hind feet help it navigate in water. Otters eat various sea life. Otter whiskers help them sense small animals in murky water, as well as avoid obstacles while swimming. Otters have small front paws, which they use to hold their food when they eat.

7. (A) (The traveler was then sent to Nottingham, where Robin's greatest foes lived.) According to myth, Robin Hood lived long ago in Sherwood Forest. Owned by England's king, the forest was actually ruled by Robin and his group. An expert archer, Robin invited any traveler through the forest to dine with him. Afterward, he asked if the traveler was in need. If so, Robin gave the traveler money. If not, Robin took the traveler's valuables. They felt Robin was a thief, but commoners felt he was a hero because he stole from the rich to provide for the poor.

(B) (The traveler was then sent to Nottingham, where Robin's greatest foes lived.) According to myth, Robin Hood lived long ago in Sherwood Forest. Owned by England's king, the forest was actually ruled by Robin and his group. An expert archer, Robin invited any traveler through the forest to dine with him. Afterward, he asked if the traveler was in need. If so, Robin gave the traveler money. If not, Robin took the traveler's valuables. They felt Robin was a thief, but commoners felt he was a hero because he stole from the rich to provide for the poor.

Unit 6
Revising

8. (A) If you ever have to speak in front of an audience, preparation is crucial. Recite your speech until you can say it without using your notes. Make sure to research your topic, and save key points on note cards. When ready, add gestures and tones of voice for emphasis. Say your speech for friends and family, and then ask for their input. With preparation, you should feel confident delivering your actual speech.

(B) If you ever have to speak in front of an audience, preparation is crucial. Recite your speech until you can say it without using your notes. Make sure to research your topic, and save key points on note cards. When ready, add gestures and tones of voice for emphasis. Say your speech for friends and family, and then ask for their input. With preparation, you should feel confident delivering your actual speech.

9. (A) The White House, the Capitol, the Pentagon, and the Supreme Court are there. Washington, D.C. has many important buildings and structures. The Washington Monument, the Lincoln Memorial, and the Jefferson Memorial are all in the nation's capital. Washington, D.C. also has an area devoted to foreign embassies.

(B) The White House, the Capitol, the Pentagon, and the Supreme Court are there. Washington, D.C. has many important buildings and structures. The Washington Monument, the Lincoln Memorial, and the Jefferson Memorial are all in the nation's capital. Washington, D.C. also has an area devoted to foreign embassies.

10. (A) Within the wide range of types of stars, the sun is between supergiants and neutron stars. The sun is the only star known to support life on a planet that revolves around it. Currently the sun is middle-aged, but it will become a red giant in about five billion years. The sun is actually a star, like billions of others in the universe.

(B) Within the wide range of types of stars, the sun is between supergiants and neutron stars. The sun is the only star known to support life on a planet that revolves around it. Currently the sun is middle-aged, but it will become a red giant in about five billion years. The sun is actually a star, like billions of others in the universe.

35

A. Exercising Your Skill

You have been learning about revising. Specifically, you have been learning about staying on topic by adding appropriate details to or removing inaccurate details from a piece of writing. You have also learned how to organize a piece of writing into its correct order. Number your paper from 1 to 10. Read each sentence below to decide if it is true or false. If the sentence is true, write the letter **T** on your paper. If the sentence is false, write the letter **F** on your paper.

1. There is only one way to revise a piece of writing.

2. The revising process does not begin until after you have written something.

3. Revising is the time to improve a piece of writing.

4. During revising, it is not important to consider the purpose of your writing.

5. All information in a piece of writing should support the main idea.

6. Making sure you stay on topic is part of the revising process.

7. Organizing a piece of writing is not part of the writing process.

8. There is no correct order in a piece of writing.

9. You do not have to consider correct order when explaining a process.

10. You do have to consider correct order when telling a story.

B. Expanding Your Skill

Number your paper from 1 to 6. Read the paragraph below. Sentences in the paragraph are *not* in the correct order. Write the letters of the sentences in the order they should appear.

(A) Daniel married Rebecca Bryan soon after moving to North Carolina. **(B)** After a life full of adventure, Daniel Boone passed away in 1820 while residing in Missouri. **(C)** In 1773 Daniel sold his North Carolina farm and made his home in Kentucky. **(D)** In 1734 Daniel Boone was born in Pennsylvania. **(E)** Having become a skilled hunter and frontiersman, Daniel began to explore the Kentucky border in 1769. **(F)** When Daniel was eighteen, he and his family moved to North Carolina.

C. Exploring Language

Descriptive Writing Number your paper from 1 to 4. Read the passage below to decide which four sentences do *not* stay on topic and should be removed. Write the letters of those sentences on your paper.

What Is a Crustacean?

(A) A crustacean is a creature that spends much of its time in water. (B) Sharks are not mammals; they are fish. (C) Most crustaceans, such as crabs, lobsters, shrimps, and crayfish, live in oceans or freshwater rivers. (D) For those crustaceans that live on land, finding a moist area to inhabit is vital to prevent them from drying out. (E) The soft, inside body of a crustacean is protected by a hard outer skeleton called an *exoskeleton.* (F) The Indian Ocean is east of Africa, west of Australia, and south of Asia. (G) Crustaceans have antennae. (H) This channel has great nature programming. (I) Similar to cat whiskers, a crustacean's antennae help them sense. (J) This way crustaceans can find food. (K) Different crustaceans eat different things. (L) A crustacean's diet can include other smaller crustaceans, scraps from another animal's meal, starfish, and plankton. (M) Whales are mammals. (N) Plankton is a barely visible combination of plant and animal life that thrives in water. (O) As crustaceans grow, they shed their exoskeletons to be replaced by new and larger ones.

D. Expressing Yourself

Choose one of these activities. When you are finished, give your paper to your teacher.

1. Explain a process or tell a story in a brief paragraph. When you finish, revise your piece of writing. Make sure the information in your paragraph stays on topic and that it is in the correct order.

2. **WORK with a PARTNER** Find a partner. Each of you should choose a newspaper or a magazine article. The article should be at least two paragraphs in length. Working separately, select one of your article's paragraphs to rewrite out of order. When both of you are done, switch papers with your partner. Then write your partner's paragraph in the order you think is correct. Together, discuss why you put the paragraph's sentences in the order you did, and then compare your work to the original.

Unit 7
Revising

Once you have made sure that your writing stays on topic and its ideas are in the correct order, you can focus on revising, or improving, your beginning and ending. Although a piece of writing's beginning can be simple, thinking about how to end it can be a challenge. Ask yourself:
- Is my beginning clear? Does it fit my purpose?
- Have I written what I wanted to say?
- Where should I end my writing?
- Is my ending clear? Does it fit my purpose?
- Does my ending make sense with my beginning?

Read each piece of writing. Then answer the questions about how to revise it.

<u>There are many insects at the zoo.</u> The shapes, patterns, and colors of leaf insects enable them to blend in with their surroundings so well that they become invisible to predators. Leaf insects look like bright green leaves. Small brown spots scattered over their bodies give the appearance that they have been nibbled. A leaf insect's swaying motion as it walks mimics a leaf waving in the breeze, thus completing its perfect camouflage. Stick insects look like dry twigs. Their long, slender legs are nearly invisible. A stick insect's body can change to the exact color of its surroundings. Some stick insects have bumps and spines that resemble twig buds or thorns. Stick insects are undetectable as they rest on trees, plants, or dry leaves on the ground. **Their eggs are even camouflaged; they resemble tiny seeds.**

1. Which sentence is a better beginning than the underlined sentence?
   (A) The zoo has many unusual creatures.
   (B) Ladybugs are reddish -orange with black spots.
   (C) Leaf insects and stick insects are masters of disguise.

2. Which sentence is a better ending than the boldfaced sentence?
   (A) Stick insects are able to grow another leg if one is bitten off by a predator.
   (B) In addition, the eggs of both leaf and stick insects are camouflaged by looking like seeds.
   (C) The zoo's insect building has different hours than the zoo's outdoor exhibits.

An arctic tern is a bird. Most will travel more than 8,000 miles. Arctic terns spend summer in different places, such as eastern Canada and northwestern Scotland. In winter, arctic terns can be found near southern Africa and near antarctic waters. These birds live in colonies as they breed and raise their young. Once young terns mature, they complete the migration without the help of their parents. **I do not know how fast an arctic tern can fly.**

3. Which sentence is a better beginning than the underlined sentence?
   (A) The arctic tern is a bird with one of the longest paths of migration.
   (B) Common terns and arctic terns look a lot alike.
   (C) Some bird species are faster than others.

4. Which sentence is a better ending than the boldfaced sentence?
   (A) A common tern is also a bird.
   (B) A colony of the same species living together provides protection.
   (C) It seems that arctic terns spend much of their time in the air.

My grandfather collects ships-in-a-bottle. Coins and stamps are common examples of items to collect. With a long history of currency in so many countries, there are plenty of ways to focus or expand a coin collection. The same applies to stamps. Different countries have a variety of stamps. Like coins, the value of stamps has a wide range. Some coins and stamps are worth more when they are rare, come from a certain era, or have been made with errors. **My aunt collects spoons.**

5. Which sentence is a better beginning than the underlined sentence?
   (A) My parents collect antique cameras.
   (B) Starting and keeping a collection can be a fun, yet busy, hobby.
   (C) It is important to keep a collection at a manageable size.

6. Which sentence is a better ending than the boldfaced sentence?
   (A) Researching collectibles is a good way to keep a hobby from becoming an obsession.
   (B) Treasures can be found at flea markets, auctions, and yard sales.
   (C) My grandmother collects quilts.

Read each piece of writing. Then answer the questions about how to revise it.

The city where my family lives has an orchestra with a sixty-year tradition. Each instrument has been mastered by its musician. An orchestra is divided into sections, each containing a specific family of instruments. There is a string section, including the cello and the harp. There is a brass section, including tubas and trumpets. Drums and bells are part of the percussion section. The woodwind family includes saxophones and oboes. **We cannot see the piano from our seats.**

7. Which sentence is a better beginning than the underlined sentence?
   (A) The conductor stands facing the orchestra.
   (B) The conductor uses a thin baton to direct the orchestra.
   (C) An orchestra's music is the result of numerous instruments.

8. Which sentence is a better ending than the boldfaced sentence?
   (A) Instruments with strings are plucked with fingers or a bow.
   (B) The majority of an orchestra is stringed instruments.
   (C) An orchestra's instruments are arranged in a way to optimize their sounds.

Many planting pots can stay outdoors year-round. The first step is preparing the clay, which happens by kneading the clay. This helps the clay to become rigid and to dry evenly. The next step is molding the clay into a pot. This is done by working slowly from the base upward to form the pot's shape. The last step is baking, or "firing," the pot. This occurs in a special oven to secure the pot's shape. **Pottery is a nice gift.**

9. Which sentence is a better beginning than the underlined sentence?
   (A) Here are the steps to make a clay pot.
   (B) Next year our garden will include eggplant, garlic, and squash.
   (C) The community college's pottery class starts in March.

10. Which sentence is a better ending than the boldfaced sentence?
    (A) Roses need to be transplanted out of their pot at a certain size.
    (B) By practicing these steps, your clay pot technique should improve.
    (C) What else can be made from clay?

Do you like to study science? The sun emits white light, which consists of all the colors in the visible light spectrum. When white light passes through a prism, the colors separate into distinct bands. Each color has its own wavelength. Red and orange have the longest wavelengths; blue and violet have the shortest wavelengths. As sunlight fills the atmosphere, most longer wavelengths go directly through it. Blue light, due to its shorter wavelength, is absorbed by gas molecules in the air. **Bodies of water often reflect the color of the sky, even when it is cloudy.**

11. Which sentence is a better beginning than the underlined sentence?
    (A) Do you know why the sky is blue?
    (B) Mixing yellow and green makes blue.
    (C) What are wavelengths?

12. Which sentence is a better ending than the boldfaced sentence?
    (A) Blue is also a color in rainbows.
    (B) How do you measure wavelengths?
    (C) The molecules then scatter the light into the atmosphere, giving the sky its blue appearance.

Sometimes curling is on television. It is thought that curling started in Scotland. In the 1700s the sport made its way to North America when Scottish soldiers fought in the French and Indian War. Curling can be explained as shuffleboard on ice. Players use a special broom to slide their "stones," which resemble tea kettles. The distance between stones is key to curling scores. **All sports are competitive.**

13. Which sentence is a better beginning than the underlined sentence?
    (A) Heat from a curling iron is what helps set the curl.
    (B) The sport of curling can be traced back to the 1500s.
    (C) Is curling an Olympic event?

14. Which sentence is a better ending than the boldfaced sentence?
    (A) The French and Indian War lasted approximately six years.
    (B) Is curling popular in Canada?
    (C) To be successful, curling requires precision and strategy.

Now that you have considered staying on topic, maintaining correct order, and writing good beginnings and endings, you can revise your writing for word choice. Choosing **exact words** helps make a piece of writing more clear.

Good: We **went** to an **exhibit** at the **museum**.

Better: We **examined** a **Medieval** exhibit at **Union Museum**.

Ask yourself the following questions as you revise for word choice.
- Does the piece of writing provide a vivid picture for the reader?
- Can more specific nouns or verbs be used?
- Can more descriptive adjectives or adverbs be used?
- Are there words that need to be explained or defined further?

Read each piece of writing. Then answer the questions about how to revise it.

Prior to 1500, there were several Native American tribes inhabiting what is now Texas. <u>In 1519 the Texas coast was explored.</u> Throughout the 1500s, various expeditions traveled through Texas. In 1685 the French began Fort St. Louis; Spaniards eventually obtained the fort when they found it deserted. In the 1700s Texas became home to more Spanish people. Battles to claim Texas filled the 1800s. Led by Sam Houston, independence was won, and the Republic of Texas was declared in 1836. This, however, did not mean that the Republic was part of the United States. The city of Austin was selected for the Republic's capital in 1839. President James Polk was instrumental in the statehood of the Republic of Texas. **It became a state.**

1. Which sentence is the most specific and would best replace the underlined sentence?
   (A) In 1519 Alonzo Alvarez de Pineda explored the Texas coast.
   (B) In 1519 a Spanish explorer arrived on the Texas coast.
   (C) In 1519 a European explorer explored the Texas coast.

2. Which sentence is the most specific and would best replace the boldfaced sentence?
   (A) Texas became a state.
   (B) It became a state in 1845.
   (C) Texas became a state in 1845.

These snakes are many colors. Burmese pythons come from Burma, Vietnam, and Thailand. One of the most common Burmese pythons is the albino Burmese python. The word *albino* refers to the lack of pigment in the snake's skin. The albino Burmese python's skin is white with yellow to orange markings. **These snakes are rare in the wild.** Depending on gender, Burmese pythons can grow to eighteen feet in length.

3. Which sentence is the most specific and would best replace the underlined sentence?
   (A) Burmese pythons are snakes that can be a variety of colors.
   (B) These are types of snakes that can have different colors.
   (C) These snakes can be a variety of colors.

4. Which sentence is the most specific and would best replace the boldfaced sentence?
   (A) Albino Burmese pythons are rare in the wild because they are seen easily by predators.
   (B) These snakes are rare in the wild because of their colors.
   (C) They are rare in the wild because they are seen easily by predators.

Born Elizabeth Griscom, Betsy Ross was the seamstress who became famous for sewing the first United States flag. She lived much of her life in Philadelphia, Pennsylvania, and came from a large family. She was one of many children. Although history is not clear about who designed the flag, it is clear that George Washington was one of the men to approach her about the flag's design. **One day, a group adopted the nation's flag.**

5. Which sentence is the most specific and would best replace the underlined sentence?
   (A) Betsy Ross was one of many children.
   (B) She was one of seventeen children.
   (C) Betsy Ross was one of seventeen children.

6. Which sentence is the most specific and would best replace the boldfaced sentence?
   (A) On June 14, 1777, an important group adopted the nation's flag.
   (B) On June 14, 1777, the Continental Congress adopted the nation's flag, and now the United States celebrates this day as Flag Day.
   (C) One day in 1777 the Continental Congress adopted the flag.

For each numbered sentence, decide which choice uses more exact wording.

(7) London is one of the cities in the world. The heart of the city is Piccadilly Circus. (8) It is not a circus; it is an area where streets intersect. Not far from Piccadilly Circus is Trafalgar Square, one of the most visited sites in London. (9) A memorial statue of some guy is in the square. Historical buildings, including the National Gallery, surround Trafalgar Square. (10) The National Gallery is a museum. (11) Another attraction is the palace. (12) Within its gates, the well-known Changing the Guard occurs. (13) This is Guard Mounting. (14) This is the time when the guards change.

7. **(A)** London is one of the largest cities in the world.
   (B) London, England, is one of the largest cities in the world.

8. **(A)** It is not a circus; it is a circular area where five busy streets intersect.
   (B) It is not a circus; it is an area where five streets intersect.

9. **(A)** A memorial statue of Admiral Nelson is in the square.
   (B) A memorial statue of some British guy is in the square.

10. **(A)** The National Gallery is a wonderful museum of art.
    (B) The National Gallery is a wonderful museum.

11. **(A)** Another attraction in London is the palace.
    (B) Another attraction in London is Buckingham Palace.

12. **(A)** Within its gates, the well-known Changing the Guard occurs on either all-even or all-odd days at 11:30 A.M.
    (B) Within its gates, the well-known Changing the Guard occurs at 11:30 A.M.

13. **(A)** This ceremony's name is Guard Mounting.
    (B) This ceremony's proper name is Guard Mounting.

14. **(A)** This is the time when the guards change shifts.
    (B) This is the time when the royal guards change shifts.

Solving a crime can be a long process. The first police officers on the scene secure the area. **(15)** The police do a lot of work. **(16)** One or more specialized officers are assigned to check into the situation. **(17)** Detectives work hard also. For those permitted to enter the crime scene, it is crucial that they wear gloves and that they bag evidence so clues are not tainted. **(18)** The stuff is given to people who research crime. Their research may lead to more accurate details about the crime. **(19)** Advances in technology help. **(20)** Once people are captured, they are questioned. **(21)** If there is enough, they are taken. **(22)** If the case goes somewhere, suspects need to be defended.

15. **(A)** The police prevent people from leaving or entering, and they make sure evidence is not disturbed.
    (B) They do a lot of work, such as making sure stuff is not touched.

16. **(A)** One or more specialized officers check into it.
    (B) One or more detectives are assigned to investigate the crime.

17. **(A)** Detectives search for clues.
    (B) Detectives examine the crime scene, search for clues, and interview witnesses.

18. **(A)** The evidence is given to specialists who research crime and criminals.
    (B) It is given to people who research crime.

19. **(A)** Advances in technology help specialists.
    (B) Advances in technology help specialists uncover what is not obvious to the naked eye.

20. **(A)** Once captured, suspects are questioned by detectives.
    (B) Once people are captured, suspects are questioned by other people.

21. **(A)** If there is enough proof, suspects are arrested.
    (B) If there is enough, suspects are taken.

22. **(A)** If the case goes to court, suspects usually have lawyers for their defense.
    (B) If the case goes to court, suspects need to be defended.

In writing, **tone** is the attitude the writer expresses. Most times, the tone reflects the writer's purpose. Here are general examples of tone:

- **Formal:** This tone is used in business letters, reports, and certain articles. It sounds serious and does *not* use contractions or slang.
- **Informal:** This tone is used in friendly letters, notes, and some stories. It sounds friendly and similar to conversation and can use slang.

More specific examples of tone are listed below. Depending on a writer's purpose, each can be used in all types of writing.

- **Factual:** This tone expresses fact and is typically formal.
- **Humor:** This tone is fun, or entertaining, and typically informal.
- **Anger:** This tone shows disappointment and is formal or informal.
- **Admiration:** This tone expresses respect and is typically formal.
- **Gratitude:** This tone shows thankfulness and is formal or informal.

As you revise, make sure all of the sentences in your piece of writing express the tone you intend.

Read each piece of writing to determine its tone.

To Whom It May Concern:

I am writing about one of your company's cordless telephones, the LX6900 model. It does not hold its charge. I have enclosed a copy of my receipt. I purchased the telephone more than ninety days ago and know that the warranty has expired. I was wondering if there is anything else your company could do. Thank you for your time.

Sincerely,

Marcus Banks

1. **(A)** admiration   **(B)** anger   **(C)** factual

Hey Sari,

    Sorry I missed you. I just wanted to thank you for the homemade bread. It went great with my apple butter. I really appreciate your thoughtfulness. Talk to you later.

Nina

2. **(A)** humor   **(B)** gratitude   **(C)** factual

I cannot believe you forgot to pick me up from the dentist's office. I was waiting for over an hour! I am mad because I had research to do for my report, and now I have less time to look for information. I would not be so mad if you had been doing something important, but you just forgot. Next time, I will be sure to call and remind you.

3. (A) admiration   **(B)** anger   **(C)** humor

Maude and Elliot constantly confuse what the other one says. For example, Elliot might say, "Are you done with that book?" And Maude might reply, "I did not give you a dirty look." Or Maude might say, "I think we should go to the park." And Elliot might reply, "Turn on a light if you think it is dark."

4. (A) humor   **(B)** gratitude   **(C)** anger

My hero is my grandpa. I love to listen to his stories, especially his experiences when he was my age. He has seen a lot in his life, and he always tells me how fulfilling it has been. I chose my grandpa as my hero because he is honest, caring, and dependable. He is also very active in his community. He is more than my grandpa; he is my friend.

5. (A) gratitude   **(B)** humor   **(C)** admiration

Our journal assignment is to write about four things for which we are thankful. The first thing I am grateful for is my family, which includes our dog Foley. I am thankful for the place where I live with my family. I am thankful that we have food to eat and water to drink. I am grateful that I go to a nice school to learn.

6. (A) gratitude   **(B)** admiration   **(C)** factual

Read each letter to answer the questions that follow.

Dear Sir or Madam:

I am writing to request information about state parks in central Colorado. **(8)** A group of us is planning a camping trip. We need help deciding where to visit. First of all, we would like to be able to ride our bikes. Which parks have bike trails? **(9)** Hiking, canoeing, and swimming are cool activities also.

Finally, we would like to know how much it costs to rent a cabin for six people. **(10)** We plan to stay a bit. Could you please send park brochures and maps to help us? I am sure you are busy, but it would be great if you could send the information within the next two weeks. **(11)** Thanks a bunch!

Sincerely,

Anita Rountree

7. What is the tone of this letter?
   (A) anger   **(B)** humor   **(C)** factual

For sentences 8, 9, 10, and 11 above, decide which choice best replaces each sentence to express the letter's tone.

8. **(A)** My friends and I are planning a summer camping trip.
   (B) A bunch of us is planning a summer camping trip.

---

9. **(A)** Hiking, canoeing, and swimming are activities we also enjoy.
   (B) Hiking, canoeing, and swimming are very cool activities.

---

10. **(A)** The group and I plan to hang out for a while.
    (B) My friends and I plan to stay for five nights.

---

11. **(A)** Thank you a bunch!
    (B) I appreciate your time and consideration.

Dear Yoshiko,

I was wrong about this camp. It's been awesome! **(13)** Next year, we should attend this interesting camp with one another. Each day has a schedule of fun stuff, even though we have to eat breakfast by 8:00 a.m. We take a lot of nature hikes. We study different bugs, birds, and plants. There is a great mushy swamp. **(14)** Perhaps if people walk softly near the swamp and remain quiet and still, a frog species will emerge.

One pal I've met here in my camp group is Meg. I think you'd really like her. She's from New York, loves horses, and tells goofy riddles. **(15)** After we eat in the afternoon, our group participates in the creation of crafts. We get to make all kinds of neat stuff, such as puzzles and collages. So, what have you been doing? **(16)** Please write back to me at your earliest convenience. I can't wait to see you!

Your friend,

Sandy

12. What is the tone of this letter?
   (A) friendly   **(B)** anger   **(C)** humor

For sentences 13, 14, 15, and 16 above, decide which choice best replaces each sentence to express the letter's tone.

13. (A) Next year, you and I should come to this camp together.
   (B) Next year, we should attend this interesting camp together.

---

14. (A) If we walk softly near the swamp and remain still, maybe we will see some species of frog.
   (B) We walk quietly near the swamp and stay still, hoping to see frogs.

---

15. (A) After lunch, our group has craft time.
   (B) After we eat in the afternoon, we participate in craft-making.

---

16. (A) Please write as soon as you can.
   (B) Please respond when you have time.

A. Exercising Your Skill

You have been continuing to learn about the process of revising. You have learned how to improve beginnings and endings, use more exact words, and recognize the tone of a piece of writing. Number your paper from 1 to 10. Read each sentence below to decide if it is true or false. If the sentence is true, write the letter **T** on your paper. If the sentence is false, write the letter **F** on your paper.

1. It is more important that only the end of a piece of writing is clear.

2. The writer's purpose does not matter to the beginning or the ending of a piece of writing.

3. In a piece of writing, it is not important to explain or define difficult words for readers.

4. Some verbs can be replaced with more specific verbs.

5. Some nouns can be replaced with more exact nouns, such as proper nouns.

6. It is important to provide a vivid picture with a piece of writing.

7. Adjectives cannot be replaced with more descriptive adjectives.

8. The tone of a piece of writing is the attitude the writer expresses.

9. Formal and informal tones are expressed the same in writing.

10. A letter of gratitude expresses thankfulness or appreciation.

B. Expanding Your Skill

Number your paper from 1 to 6. Read the sentences below. Replace each underlined word with a more exact word from the box.

beats	padded	instruments	friendly	music	strums

1. Our new music teacher is <u>nice</u>.

2. He plays many <u>objects</u>.

3. He <u>plays</u> the guitar.

4. He <u>uses</u> the drums.

5. Our music room has <u>special</u> walls.

6. The walls prevent our <u>sounds</u> from disturbing other classes.

C. Exploring Language

Narrative Writing Number your paper from 1 to 4. Read the passage below to decide which sentences do *not* express the factual tone that the writer intended. Write the letters of those sentences on your paper.

(A) After the Gold Rush of 1849, the population of California just totally went out of control. (B) Departing from St. Louis, Missouri, mail that was destined for California arrived in San Francisco by stagecoach. (C) To reduce the delivery time of mail between these two cities, the Pony Express was introduced in 1860. (D) It blows my mind to think that a one-way trip of the Pony Express took about six weeks. (E) Pony Express riders rode in relays, which means one rider would meet the next rider on another horse to continue the mail's journey. (F) Riders traveled approximately seventy-five miles per day. (G) The Pony Express included about eighty horseback riders. (H) They better have taken good care of those horses! (I) The Pony Express was able to complete the St. Louis-to-San Francisco journey in eight days. (J) After less than two years, however, the invention of the telegraph made the Pony Express unnecessary. (K) I'm sure the ponies were thankful for that!

D. Expressing Yourself

Choose one of these activities. When you are finished, give your paper to your teacher.

1. Think of something helpful or nice that someone did for you. Or, think of a different positive event that you experienced. Remember what you learned about the tone of a piece of writing. Using the tone of gratitude, write a short letter or a paragraph expressing your thankfulness to that person or about that event.

2. **WORK with a PARTNER** With a partner, think of an idea for a short story. The story can be true or make-believe, such as a heroic rescue or the legend of a kingdom you create. After you choose the idea for your story, decide together what tone the story should have. Remember that specific tones include admiration, humor, gratitude, factual, and anger. Write your short story. Take time to revise the story together, and make sure that the tone you intended is maintained.

After revising, it is time to **edit,** or **proofread,** your writing. This is when you make your writing correct, such as fixing errors in spelling, grammar, usage, and mechanics. Here are some questions to consider:

- Are words spelled correctly?
- Are capital letters used correctly?
- Are the correct punctuation marks used?
- Is correct grammar used? For example, subjects and verbs should agree.
- Are extra or repeated words and unnecessary spaces removed?
- Have rules of usage been followed? Here are a few common errors:

Incorrect: It rained **alot**.	Correct: It rained **a lot**.
Incorrect: She swims **good**.	Correct: She swims **well**.
Incorrect: **There's** many errors.	Correct: **There are** many errors.
Incorrect: I **use to** shop there.	Correct: I **used to** shop there.

As you edit, always make sure the assignment's goals have been met.

Choose the sentence that has been edited.

1. (A) Please let me know when you finishe your homework.
   (B) Please let me know when you finish your homework.
   (C) Please let me know when you finish you're homework.

2. (A) Those horses are arabian stallions.
   (B) Those horses are arabian Stallions.
   (C) Those horses are Arabian stallions.

3. (A) Havasu Falls is some of the most lovely waterfalls in North America.
   (B) Havasu Falls is some of the more lovely waterfalls in North America.
   (C) Havasu Falls is one of the most lovely waterfalls in North America.

4. (A) This canoe trip was a new experience for my sisters and me.
   (B) This canoe trip was a new experience for my sisters and me?
   (C) This canoe trip was a new experience for my sister's and me.

5. (A) People throughout the world enjoys playing sports.
   (B) People throughout the world enjoy play sports.
   (C) People throughout the world enjoy playing sports.

6. **(A)** My Aunt Aunt Francesca sent me a sweater for my birthday.
   (B) My Aunt Francesca sent me a sweater for my birthday.
   (C) My aunt Francesca sent me a sweater for my birthday.

7. **(A)** The family sat on the patio, but they ran into the house when lightning struck nearby.
   (B) The family sat on the patio; but they ran into the house when lightning struck.
   (C) The family sat on the patio but they ran into the house when lightning struck.

8. **(A)** Although it is not the capital, alot of people live in New York City.
   (B) Although it is not the capital, a lots of people live in New York City.
   (C) Although it is not the capital, a lot of people live in New York City.

9. **(A)** Are the textbooks your's or his?
   (B) Are the textbooks yours' or his'?
   (C) Are the textbooks yours or his?

10. **(A)** "This is the last stop, announced the bus driver."
   (B) "This is the last stop," announced the bus driver.
   (C) "This is the last stop", announced the bus driver.

11. **(A)** On Wednesdays, I practice the flute.
   (B) On Wensdays, I practice the flute.
   (C) On wednesdays, I practice the flute.

12. **(A)** That was the greatest show I have ever seen!
   (B) That was the greatest show I have ever seen
   (C) That was the greatest show I have ever seen?

13. **(A)** Make sure to use these items tweezers, a dropper, and a microscope slide.
   (B) Make sure to use these items, tweezers, a dropper, and a microscope slide.
   (C) Make sure to use these items: tweezers, a dropper, and a microscope slide.

Choose the sentence that has been edited.

14. **(A)** Raoul use to live in Bismarck, North Dakota.
    (B) Raoul used to live in Bismarck, North Dakota.
    (C) Raoul used live in Bismarck, North Dakota.

15. **(A)** The japanese language uses characters rather than letters.
    (B) The Japanese Language uses characters rather than letters.
    (C) The Japanese language uses characters rather than letters.

16. **(A)** Several socer teams are staying at the new hotel for this weekend's tournament.
    (B) Several soccerr teams are staying at the new hotel for this weekend's tournament.
    (C) Several soccer teams are staying at the new hotel for this weekend's tournament.

17. **(A)** What is the most thrilling roller coaster you have ever ridden?
    (B) What is the most thrilling roller coaster you have ever ridden.
    (C) What is the most thrilling roller coaster you have ever ridden!

18. **(A)** I think that building is going to be an Italian restaurant, said Melanie.
    (B) "I think that building is going to be an Italian restaurant," said Melanie.
    (C) I think that building is going to be an Italian restaurant, said Melanie."

19. **(A)** The dry brown leaves falled to the ground.
    (B) The dry, brown leaves fell to the ground.
    (C) The dry, brown leafs fell to the ground.

20. **(A)** The boys plays at the park until it closes.
    (B) The boys playing at the park until it closes.
    (C) The boys play at the park until it closes.

21. (A) Kellys' dog is playful and well-behaved.
(B) Kellys dog is playful and well-behaved.
(C) Kelly's dog is playful and well-behaved.

22. (A) History is a difficult subject for me, but I still try to do more good.
(B) History is a difficult subject for me, but I still try to do good.
(C) History is a difficult subject for me, but I still try to do well.

23. (A) He cannot drive nowhere until we find the car keys.
(B) He cannot drive anywhere until we find the car keys.
(C) He cannot drive anywheres until we find the car keys.

24. (A) Mr Perez, a librarian, kindly asked us to be quiet.
(B) Mr. Perez, a librarian, kindly asked us "to be quiet."
(C) Mr. Perez, a librarian, kindly asked us to be quiet.

25. (A) The president himself did not write the speech he delivered to Congress.
(B) The president him did not write the speech he delivered to Congress.
(C) The president hisself did not write the speech he delivered to Congress.

26. (A) Soaring above the tall grass, a mouse was spied by the eagle.
(B) Soaring above the tall grass, the eagle spied a mouse.
(C) Soaring above the tall grass the eagle spied a mouse.

27. (A) In this forest, the least dangerous path is also the shortest path.
(B) In this forest, the lesser dangerous path is also the shortest path.
(C) In this forest, the lest dangerous path is also the shortest path.

28. (A) The class did good on their exam.
(B) The class did on their exam.
(C) The class did well on their exam.

Unit 11
Editing/Proofreading

As you edit your writing, **proofreading marks** can be used to label errors. They are special marks to show where certain mistakes occur.

- Use ∧ to add something other than a period.

    They're here. ⟶ They're here.

- Use ⊙ to add a period.

    Many bugs fly⊙ ⟶ Many bugs fly.

- Use ⟍ᵞ to remove something.

    The moon ~~moon~~ is full. ⟶ The moon is full.

- Use ⬭ to show that a word is misspelled.

    Is he ⟨reddie⟩? ⟶ Is he ready?

Read each sentence. Then choose the sentence that has been corrected based on the proofreading marks.

1. My brother likes to ride his ~~his~~ bicycle as I skateboard.

    (A) My brother likes to ride his bicycle as I skateboard.
    (B) My brother likes to ride his his. bicycle as I skateboard.
    (C) My brother likes to ride his his' bicycle as I skateboard.

2. The five Great Lakes make up the largest freshwater system in the world.

    (A) The Great five Lakes make up the largest freshwater system in the world.
    (B) The five Great Lakes make up the largest freshwater system in the world.
    (C) The five Lakes make up the largest freshwater system in the world.

3. Is Ray Bradbury an ⟨auther⟩?

    (A) Is Ray Bradbury an authur?
    (B) Is Ray Bradbury an auther.
    (C) Is Ray Bradbury an author?

4. My family moved here from Chicago when I was six years old⊙

(A) My family moved here from Chicago when I was six years old!
(B) My family moved here from Chicago when I was six years old?
(C) My family moved here from Chicago when I was six years old.

5. During⁄the Memorial Day parade, many veterans participated by wearing their uniforms.

(A) During the, Memorial Day parade, many veterans participated by wearing their uniforms.
(B) During the Memorial Day parade, many veterans participated by wearing their uniforms.
(C) During. the Memorial Day parade, many veterans participated by wearing their uniforms.

6. Would you like to go on an Alaskan cruise?

(A) Would you like to go on an Alaskan cruise?
(B) Would you like to go on an Alaskan cruise.
(C) Would you like to go on an Alaskan cruise!

7. Elephantes use their trunks for many purposes.

(A) Elephant use their trunks for many purposes.
(B) Elephants use their trunks for many purposes.
(C) Elephantess use their trunks for many purposes.

8. We would have been on time but there was traffic.

(A) We would have been on time; but there was traffic.
(B) We would have been on time. But there was traffic.
(C) We would have been on time, but there was traffic.

9. This apple cider is too tart for me to drink⊙

(A) This apple cider is too tart for me to drink.
(B) This apple cider is too tart for me to drink?
(C) This apple cider is too tart for me to drinks

Here are more proofreading marks to use as you edit.

- Use ≡ to show that a letter should be capitalized.

    Where is Mrs. patel? ⟶ Where is Mrs. Patel?
    ‗‗

- Use ⁄ to show that a letter should be lowercase.

    DR. Royce is late. ⟶ Dr. Royce is late.

- Use ⅄ to add a space.

    The lily isblooming. ⟶ The lily is blooming.

- Use ⌒ to close up a space.

    The paint brush is dry. ⟶ The paintbrush is dry.

- Use ∿ to switch the order of letters or words.

    Please the wash car. ⟶ Please wash the car.

Read each sentence. Then choose the sentence that has been corrected based on its proofreading marks.

10. My grandparents like to visit australia.
                                    ‗‗

    (A) My grandparents like to visitaustralia.
    (B) My grandparents like to visit Australia.
    (C) My grandparents like to visit australiA.

---

11. Our team practice showcased talented many players.

    (A) Our team practice showcased talent ed many players.
    (B) Our team practice showcased Talented many players.
    (C) Our team practice showcased many talented players.

---

12. Your Boots are drying in the garage.

    (A) Your are drying in the garage.
    (B) Your BOOTS are drying in the garage.
    (C) Your boots are drying in the garage.

---

13. The video tape is due back to the library.

    (A) The videotape is due back to the library.
    (B) The video is due back to the library.
    (C) The tape is due back to the library.

14. Please address the envelope to Y.Lee.

    (A) Please address the envelope Y.lee.
    (B) Please address the envelope to Y. Lee.
    (C) Please address the envelope to YLee.

15. In africa, gazelles live in herds.

    (A) In Africa, gazelles live in herds.
    (B) In aFrica, gazelles live in herds.
    (C) In a frica, gazelles live in herds.

16. Who owns that huge cabin over looking the lake?

    (A) Who owns that huge cabin overlooking the lake?
    (B) Who owns that huge cabin over lookingthe lake?
    (C) Who owns that huge cabinover looking the lake?

17. The FBI is a Government agency.

    (A) The fbi is a Government agency.
    (B) The FBI is a Government Agency.
    (C) The FBI is a government agency.

18. Can find someone Portugal on the wall map?

    (A) Can someone find Portugal on the wall map?
    (B) Find can someone Portugal on the wall map?
    (C) Can find Portugal someone on the wall map?

19. eric excels in a variety of hobbies.

    (A) EriC excels in a variety of hobbies.
    (B) Eric excels in a variety of hobbies.
    (C) ERIC excels in a variety of hobbies.

20. Brenda and her sister look a like.

    (A) Brenda and her sister lookalike.
    (B) Brenda and her sister looka like.
    (C) Brenda and her sister look alike.

Unit 12
Publishing

Now that you have edited your writing, it is time to **publish** it. At this time, you share your writing with your planned audience, such as family, classmates, teachers, and friends. This is also the time to add final touches, including photos, drawings, graphs, charts, or other visuals. In addition to final written drafts, publishing can include oral presentation. Other options for your work are displaying or mailing it, sending it to a magazine or a newspaper, binding it into a book or a pamphlet, performing it, and sharing it electronically. Sometimes how you publish depends on your assignment.

Which publishing idea best matches each writing assignment?

Writing Assignment	Publishing Idea
1. a poem for a friend's birthday	(A) design a flyer to post around your neighborhood
2. a complaint to the mayor about street flooding where you live	(B) display your information in the school cafeteria
3. a message to a classmate about homework you missed while absent	(C) add a photo of you with your friend, and frame your work with it
4. an advertisement about doing yard work to earn money	(D) send an e-mail message
5. a story you wrote to read to one of your school's kindergarten classes	(E) record what you observe in a science journal
6. a poster about a new study club you are starting	(F) list the ingredients and steps on a note card
7. a report on the results of mold growth	(G) type a letter, and mail it in an envelope
8. a recipe of your family's strudel to give to a friend	(H) add drawings to the story, and make it into a book

Writing Assignment	Publishing Idea
9. a narrative about a family vacation	**(A)** list the steps on lined paper with helpful sketches
10. a card to thank a zookeeper who visited your class	**(B)** key it on a computer, and download corresponding moon images
11. an explanation of how to plant and grow potatoes	**(C)** type a letter, and mail it in an envelope
12. a summary about the discovery of moons near Jupiter	**(D)** include a photograph from the trip with your story
13. a request to a museum for information about an exhibit	**(E)** key it on a computer for your school newspaper
14. a fable that you wrote	**(F)** read aloud your story to classmates
15. a survey with results of your classmates' favorite foods	**(G)** use a chart or a graph to share the results
16. a news article about the school volleyball team's district win	**(H)** write a thank-you card, and mail it in an envelope
17. a history report about an inventor	**(I)** type the report, and add interesting visuals
18. a classified ad to sell large furniture items	**(J)** use a spreadsheet or lined paper to list guest information
19. a list of party guests with addresses and phone numbers	**(K)** write descriptions neatly on a note card to send to local newspapers
20. a message to a classmate about a school field trip's schedule	**(L)** send an e-mail message

The Last LAP
Language Activity Pages

A. Exercising Your Skill

You have been learning about the final steps of the writing process, including how to use certain proofreading marks and how to share your final written product. You have also learned about some things to look for while editing a piece of writing. Number your paper from 1 to 10. Read each sentence below to decide if it is true or false. If the sentence is true, write the letter **T** on your paper. If the sentence is false, write the letter **F** on your paper.

1. Editing is the part of the writing process when you make your writing correct.

2. Correcting grammar and usage errors is not important when editing.

3. Revising is the last step of the writing process.

4. Always look for spelling and punctuation errors while editing.

5. Do not worry if letters are not capitalized correctly when editing.

6. Proofreading marks can be used to label certain errors.

7. Use proofreading marks while you edit a piece of writing.

8. Proofreading marks are not helpful when labeling writing errors.

9. Publishing is the last step of the writing process.

10. During publishing, you share the final draft of your work with others.

B. Expanding Your Skill

Number your paper from 1 to 8. The errors below are labeled with proofreading marks. Which answer choice shows each error corrected?

1. week end	**(A)** week End	**(B)** weekend
2. yogert	**(A)** yo gert	**(B)** yogurt
3. Mr. carnes	**(A)** Mr. Carnes	**(B)** Mr. CARNES
4. The Dily News	**(A)** The Daily News	**(B)** The a Dily News
5. MissKim	**(A)** Miss Kim	**(B)** Misskim
6. Are sure you?	**(A)** Are sure? You	**(B)** Are you sure?
7. we'll	**(A)** we'll	**(B)** we''ll
8. Rio Grande	**(A)** Rio Grande	**(B)** RiO grande